CONTENTS

Dear Reader

Does your teacher expect you to know everything there is to know about animals and plants: How they reproduce, how they grow, how they move about and what they like to eat? (Okay, plants don't run around, but parts of them do move. Anyway, you'll find out more about that in the following pages.)

'So that's what she means!'

She does! I thought so. Well don't despair because this book has been written especially for you. 'For me?' I hear you say. Well yes, it really has been written with you in mind. It contains many of the essential, or key facts that you need to know to make your teacher think that you are the most amazing science super brain on this planet. (This may be a slight exaggeration but it certainly will help you get to grips with the world of animals and plants.) So, what are you waiting for, start reading...

NUTTY
NATURE

ROSIE McCORMICK

To Anna, with love

Chrysalis Children's Books
An imprint of Chrysalis Books Group Plc
The Chrysalis Building, Bramley Road, London W10 6SP

Paperback edition first published in 2004

Copyright © Chrysalis Books Group Plc 2002
Text by Rosie McCormick

Editor: Veronica Ross
Designer: Sarah Goodwin
Illustrator: Woody
Consultant: John Stevenson

ISBN 1 84138 181 0 (hb)
ISBN 1 84138 738 X (pb)

British Library Cataloguing in Publication Data for this
book is available from the British Library.

Printed In China

Some of the more unfamiliar words used in this book
are explained in the glossary on pages 46 and 47.

INTRODUCTION

Did you know that all life forms on this planet are made up of tiny cells? That includes all kinds of animals, including humans, as well as every kind of plant. 'And what exactly are cells I hear you mutter?'

Well, cells are individual pieces of living matter that take in energy and use it to grow and to live. Some living things have just one cell while others, like animals, have billions of them. So, cells are the building blocks of all life forms on earth.

Next, all living things, and of course that includes animals, need to breathe. And, they also need food, or nutrition. Once they have food they can make the energy they need to move, to grow and to reproduce. Finally, living things have senses. Their senses help them to respond to and survive in the world in which they live. So, these are the factors that make life on planet earth possible.

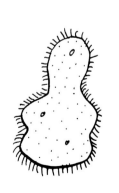

one cell

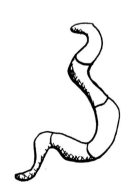

worm (not very many cells)

you (billions of cells!)

UNDERSTANDING ANIMALS

N ow because there are so many different animals (including us) scientists have developed a way to help us identify and understand animals more easily. To begin with they divided all living things into two groups, plants and animals. Then they split animals into two groups called vertebrates and invertebrates.

There are so many animals in the world, how on earth can I keep track of them all?

vertebrates

invertebrates

plants

animals

living things

Animals with backbones are called vertebrates and animals without backbones are called invertebrates. And invertebrates make up 90 per cent of all animal species.

VERTEBRATES...
Animals that have similar physical characteristics are placed into groups. Each group has a special name. The animals in the following groups are all vertebrates.

AMPHIBIANS
Amphibians are cold-blooded animals. This means that their body temperature is affected by weather conditions. (If it is hot they warm up and if it is cold they cool down.) Their skin is often thin and looks a little slimy. Can you guess what kinds of creatures belong to this class? You're right, frogs and toads.

REPTILES

Reptiles are cold blooded, too, but instead of slimy-looking skin they have scales. Their legs tend to stick out from the side of their bodies. Tortoises and turtles belong to this group and snakes do as well, although they don't have legs.

BIRDS

You probably know this already... birds have wings, feathers, two legs and a beak!

What do you get if you join three-fifths of a chick, two-thirds of a cat and half a goat?
Chicago

FISH

Fish live in water. They usually have scales and breathe through gills. Many kinds of fish have bony skeletons but some, such as sharks, have gristly skeletons.

MAMMALS

Mammals, such as dogs and rabbits, feed their babies on milk produced by the mother. All mammals are warm-blooded (this means they control their own body temperature). They have lungs and breathe air, and they all have a backbone. Guess what, we're mammals too!

... AND INVERTEBRATES

Invertebrates are animals without a backbone. Animals in this group include arachnids (such as spiders), insects and molluscs (such as such as snails and slugs).

REPRODUCTION

Animals have been around for millions of years – and plants for even longer! They have survived by reproducing themselves. If they cannot or do not reproduce their numbers will decrease and eventually they will die out or become extinct. In order for animals to reproduce, a male and a female must get together and mate. But how do animals go about finding a suitable partner? Well, different kinds of animals have their own unique methods of meeting a member of the opposite sex. Here are just a few examples.

COURTING COUPLES

When the male fiddler crab wants to attract a female, he waves a large pincer backwards and forwards in the air.

Male peacocks show off their magnificent feathers.

Humpback whales sing loud, sad songs that can be heard for hundreds of kilometres.

Male stags fight each other in front of females. Their antlers clash together as they try to prove who is the strongest.

MATING

If courting has been successful, a male and female of the same species will mate and reproduce offspring. How do they do this? Well, first a female animal produces cells called eggs and a male produces cells called sperm. When eggs and sperm join together offspring are created.

GIVING BIRTH

Mammals give birth to live young. Birds, reptiles and most fish and insects lay eggs. But of course there are always exceptions. Although the platypus is a mammal it lays eggs. And some mammals called marsupials give birth to young that are not fully developed. Young marsupials crawl into a pouch on their mother's stomach where they continue to grow.

What do you get if you cross a cocker spaniel, a poodle and a rooster?
A cockerpoodledo!

A baby kangaroo stays in its mother's pouch for about eight months.

Newborn piglets drink milk from their mother.

Ducks sit on their eggs to keep them warm until they hatch.

NUTRITION

All animals need to eat and each animal has a favourite type of food. Some animals only eat plants. They are called herbivores. Others only eat meat. They are called carnivores. And omnivores eat plants and meat. (Guess what we are?) Most animals live in an environment where the food they like to eat is close by.

FOOD CHAINS

All living things depend on each other to survive – even plants, because animals help plants to grow by depositing plant seeds in their droppings. These seeds grow into new plants. In a food chain, energy in the form of food is passed between different life forms. Each life form holds an important place in the chain.

 Producers are the first link in the chain. Plants are producers – they make their own food.

Consumers come next. Consumers are animals. They cannot make their own food and so they must look for it. Consumers eat plants or other animals.

 Predators are animals that eat other animals. They cannot make their own food. The animals they eat are called prey.

Larger predators feed on smaller predators and so on.

10

producer   consumer   small predator   large predator

In this food chain, the cabbage is food for the caterpillar. The caterpillar is food for the thrush, and the thrush is food for the cat. The cabbage is the producer and the caterpillar, thrush and cat are all consumers.

GETTING TO GRIPS WITH FOOD

Animals' teeth are perfectly suited to the kinds of food they eat. If you look inside an animal's mouth and examine its teeth you can figure out what it eats.

Carnivores, such as lions, have sharp teeth called canines at the front of their mouths for stabbing or catching their prey. They have scissor-like teeth at the back of their mouths for tearing meat.

Herbivores, like this rabbit, have strong, wide molars for munching and grinding plants.

Rodents, such as rats, have sharp incisor teeth for chewing – well just about anything.

Birds have sharp beaks for stabbing and tearing.

11

Animal Adaptations

Over thousands, even millions of years, most living things have changed or adapted in some way in order to survive in a particular environment. Animals' teeth have gradually changed shape to allow them to eat the foods they find in the parts of the world they live in. Animals have changed size, shape and even colour to become better suited to a climate, food source or even as a form of defence. The fact that animals (and plants) have adapted, and continue to adapt has helped them survive for such a long time.

Fish are adapted to life in water. Their streamlined shape and powerful fins help them move quickly through water.

Camels can live in dry places because they can go for a long time without water.

Why does a giraffe have such a long neck? Because its head is so far from its body.

Desert Survival

The tiny kangaroo rat that lives in North America is a good example of animal adaptation. It has learned to survive in harsh desert conditions. How has it done this? Well, for one thing,

it does not drink. The kangaroo rat gets moisture from the seeds it eats. Its body has evolved so that it can survive this way. And the kangaroo rat discovered that by digging underground burrows it could protect itself from the hot sun. So it has learned to survive well in an unlikely place.

DIFFERENT HABITATS

The place where an animal lives is its habitat. An animal's habitat has a particular climate, plant life and animal life. Some animals can live in different kinds of habitat, but most live in the one that suits them best.

Teacher: Name one animal that lives in Lapland.
Pupil: A reindeer.
Teacher: Good. Now name another one.
Pupil: Another reindeer.

ANIMALS ON THE MOVE

When the weather becomes too cold, and there is not enough to eat, some animals go to sleep and spend the winter months in hibernation. Others move to warmer places where there is lots of food to eat. This is called migration.

Birds are able to travel long distances and tend to fly south for the winter. Ducks, geese, swallows and swifts take to the sky in autumn. They find their way by following the sun during the day, and the moon and the stars at night.

UNDERSTANDING PLANTS

Now let's find out about plants. We have already looked at the characteristics shared by plants and animals. Now let's examine the differences between them. Although plants, like animals, are made up of cells, plant cells are different from animal cells. Plant cells are specially designed to enable them to make their own food. In other words a plant makes all the food it needs. It doesn't have to go off hunting or drive to the supermarket. Its body is a little food factory. (I'll explain exactly how they do this later.)

And, perhaps most importantly, without plants animals could not live on this planet. Not only are plants a main source of food for all kinds of animals, but they also provide oxygen without which living creatures could not breathe.

TYPES OF PLANTS

Remembering the different types of plants is not as difficult as remembering the different classes of animals. That's because all plants fall into two main categories:

Flowering plants, which can be easily identified by their brightly coloured petals.

Non-flowering plants, for example mosses, ferns and horsetails.

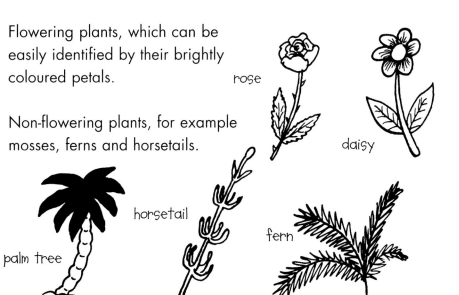

rose

daisy

horsetail

palm tree

fern

FLOWERING PLANTS

Like animals, a flowering plant's main function is to reproduce and create new plants. And, also like animals, flowering plants have male and female cells which join together to create a new flowering plant. The male parts of the flower are the stamens. Each stamen also has a part called an anther and a part called a filament. The anther produces pollen. The female parts are the carpel, stigma and style. The ovary contains the female cells.

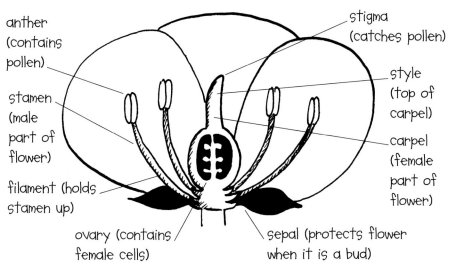

anther (contains pollen)

stamen (male part of flower)

filament (holds stamen up)

ovary (contains female cells)

stigma (catches pollen)

style (top of carpel)

carpel (female part of flower)

sepal (protects flower when it is a bud)

POLLINATION

One of a flowering plant's most important jobs is to bring about pollination so that the seeds needed for reproduction can be produced. For pollination to occur pollen, which contains the male cells, has to travel from the male part of a flower (the anther) to the female part (the stigma) of another flower of the same species. Pollen can be carried by the wind or by water, even by birds and bats, but the most important pollinators of all are insects.

Flowering plants have different ways of encouraging insects to visit them. Some have brightly coloured petals, others smell wonderful, but most attract insects with food in the form of nectar. And, as an insect drinks the nectar, pollen from the anthers sticks to the insect's body. When the insect visits another (suitable) flower, it carries with it the precious pollen. Pheeewww! This process is called cross-pollination.

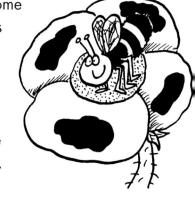

SELF—POLLINATION

But, as always, there are exceptions to every rule. There are some plants that have both male and female parts and can pollinate themselves. This is called self-pollination.

What is worse than being a fool?
Fooling with a bee?

FERTILIZATION

Finally, when a pollen grain comes into contact with a ready and waiting stigma it begins to produce a tiny tube which grows down inside the flower until it reaches the embryo sac.

Male cells travel down the
tube to meet female cells –
and new life begins again
in the form of a seed.
This process is known
as fertilization.

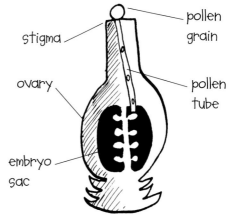

stigma

pollen
grain

ovary

pollen
tube

embryo
sac

GERMINATION

The seed contains the
beginning of a new plant.
Once the seed has been
produced it needs a suitable
environment to grow in.
A place where there is
space, light and moisture.
And when the conditions
are right, a seed will take in
water and begin to grow.
Germination happens when
the seeds start to grow.

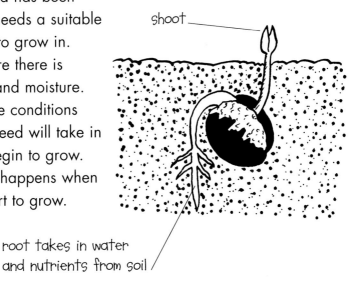

shoot

root takes in water
and nutrients from soil

Now on to the reproduction of non-flowering plants.
Don't worry, this is a much less complicated business.

NON-FLOWERING PLANTS

Non-flowering plants do not produce seeds. Instead most
reproduce by dropping spores. The spores are carried
away from the parent plant by the wind, water and animals.
A single spore is made up of cells, which will develop, in
the right conditions, into an exact copy of the parent plant.

NUTRITION

As you know, plants do not need to search for food because almost all plants make their own. They do this by using their leaves to trap the sun's energy. This process is called photosynthesis, which mean using light to make food.

This is how it works. A pigment in green plant leaves called chlorophyll absorbs sunlight. The sunlight gives the plant energy to change carbon dioxide (from the air) and water (from the ground) into a food called glucose. Plants need glucose to make starch, cellulose and to help them grow.

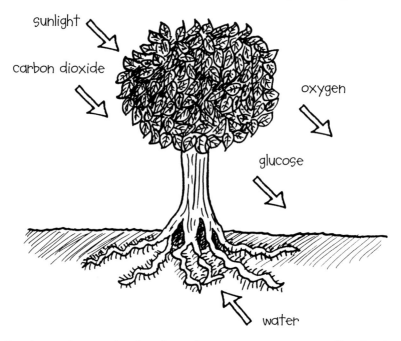

But how does a leaf collect the sun's energy? Well a leaf contains thousands of little structures called chloroplasts. Chloroplasts are like tiny solar panels that attract the sun and store up its energy until it is needed.

During photosynthesis oxygen is produced. Animals need to breathe oxygen to stay alive, so without plants there would be no living things on our planet.

DISPERSAL (SEEDS ON THE MOVE)

Animals move to find food, shelter and a mate – and so do plants. Well plants don't really move, but their seeds do. In fact, it's important that a plant's seeds find a place, preferably away from the parent plant, with enough food and light so that they can grow into strong adult plants. This is called dispersal.

sycamore seeds are carried by the wind

Plants have some clever ways of ensuring that their seeds are dispersed. Some plants have exploding seed pods which fling the seeds into the air. Others have wing-like seeds designed to be carried by the wind. While others are ideally suited to floating along rivers, and even in oceans, until they reach a new home.

dandelion seeds drift in the breeze to new ground

coconuts bob in the ocean waves to distant shores

animals feasting on fruit disperse seeds in their droppings

Animals play an important part in seed dispersal too. Some plants have fruits with hooks that can become attached to animal fur. The animal carries the stowaway for kilometres until it drops to the ground. And animals that have eaten a variety of fruits and berries release the seeds of the plants back into the earth in their droppings.

QUIZ TIME

Now just to make sure that you've been paying attention here's a little quiz to test your memory.

Fred: I can lift an elephant with one hand.
Bob: I bet you can't.
Fred: Find me an elephant with one hand and I'll show you.

1 Is a snake
a) a mammal?
b) an arachnid?
c) a reptile?

2 Are frogs hot or cold-blooded?

3 What are animals with backbones called?

4 What kind of animals lay eggs?

5 What do herbivores eat?
a) plants
b) bangers and mash
c) insects

6 Carnivores have sharp teeth in the front of their mouths, what are they called?
a) adenoids
b) canines
d) cartilage

7 What are the two main categories of plants?

8 What do most non-flowering plants produce instead of seeds?
a) branches
b) spores
c) pineapples

9 What is the name of the food produced by flowers that insects like to eat?
a) honey
b) nectar
c) jam sandwiches

10 What is the special pigment in a leaf called?
a) cellulose
b) chlorophyll
c) chloroform

11 What is a predator?

12 Why do some animals hibernate?

ANSWERS

Tom's summer with Muncher

'Tom I can't believe you volunteered to look after Muncher for the summer. You don't even like animals that much,' said Anna, Tom's twin sister.

'I DO like them,' Tom replied. 'I just don't know that much about them.'

'EXACTLY! You don't have the faintest idea how to care for this rabbit,' said Anna, as she poked her finger through the wire mesh door of the hutch and scratched Muncher's head. 'Just don't expect me to help you, that's all.' And with a flourish, Anna marched out of the kitchen leaving Tom and Muncher alone together.

IT'S A FACT
Rabbits are mammals. All mammals are warm-blooded and most have fur or hair on their bodies.

Tom sat at the kitchen table and peered into the hutch which contained the animal that had just become his sole responsibility. Somehow, and he wasn't quite sure how, he had managed to give his third-year teacher, Miss Kershaw, the impression that he more than anyone wanted to take Muncher, the English lop rabbit, home for the summer.

Tom sighed as he relived the moment when his hand shot up in response to Miss Kershaw's question. 'Now who would like to look after Muncher?' she had asked with a radiant smile on her face. Tom, along with ten other class members, captivated by this smile, immediately volunteered. But as Tom had never been chosen to do anything for Miss Kershaw before, he was confident that he would not be chosen now.

'Tom, would you like to take the little darling home?' Miss Kershaw had asked him.

IT'S A FACT
Rabbits are herbivores. That means they eat only vegetables.

Tom had simply nodded. In fact he had carried on nodding until his friend Freddy Foster elbowed him to stop. Tom had been rendered speechless by the fact that Miss Kershaw knew he existed. And so Muncher was his for six long weeks.

Tom sighed and moved his face closer to the furry creature in the hutch. 'I suppose you want something to eat,' he said. 'Well, how about some pizza?'

Next morning Tom woke suddenly to the sound of his dad's ancient lawnmower putt-putting across the lawn in the back garden.

'Oh great,' thought Tom to himself as he sat up in bed and rubbed his eyes. 'That madman is at it again!' To confirm his view that his dad needed professional help, Tom stood on the edge of the bed and peered out through the bedroom window. As he suspected, the light outside was shadowy and grey. It was early, very early. But for some reason, Tom's dad seemed to think that these were ideal grass-cutting conditions. And because their next door neighbour, Mr Benson, was slightly hard of hearing, he never complained about this odd behaviour.

Tom threw himself back on his pillow. As he began to contemplate the six weeks of absolute freedom that lay ahead, a smile swept across his face. 'No more homework, spelling quizzes or end of term tests,' thought Tom. 'In fact, I don't have a thing to worry about!'

24

Tom was still making a checklist of all the things he didn't have to do over the summer holidays, when the sound of his mother's voice wafted into his room.

'Tom, you'd better come here. I think this rabbit of yours is hungry,' Tom's mother called from the bottom of the stairs.

'Rabbit. I haven't got a rabbit,' Tom yelled back.

'Well, if it's not a rabbit, I'd like to know what it is,' replied Tom's mum.

And then it dawned on him.

'Muncher,' Tom whispered to himself.

Tom dragged himself out of bed and padded down the stairs. In the kitchen his mother was, as usual, juggling a number of household chores. Tom watched in amazement as she attempted to hold a telephone and a cup of coffee in one hand and a huge pile of dirty washing in the other.

On the hob, dad's bacon and eggs were looking rather well done and Tom sensed that burnt toast was about to appear by way of a grand finale.

Tom plodded across the kitchen floor to Muncher's hutch and gazed in at his furry friend. Muncher gazed back, occasionally twitching his nose.

IT'S A FACT
Wild brown rabbits have a better chance of survival than white or black ones. That's because their colour helps them to blend in easily with their environment.

25

'Mum tells me you're hungry. I could make you some scrambled eggs,' Tom said with a grin.

'Eggs! Rabbits do not eat eggs, sawdust brain,' chortled Anna.

Tom looked up to see his sister sitting at the kitchen table, pouring a bowl of cereal with one hand and scribbling on a piece of paper with the other.

'I know that! I was just joking,' Tom replied. As he spoke he spotted the uneaten pizza lying in the corner of the hutch. 'Hmnnn,' thought Tom. 'We'll have to get you something you do like.'

'Here. This is a list of the foods Muncher will eat,' said Anna, through a mouthful of coco puffs. 'Your pocket money should just about cover it.'

'Pocket money. I'm not paying...' began Tom.

'Oh yes you are!' said Tom's dad, taking up his position at the kitchen table.

Tom picked up the list which was written in his sister's sickeningly neat handwriting. He read:

Rabbit Food

Okay puke face, this is what you need to know.

- Rabbits should have two good meals a day. One meal should be vegetables, the other should be cereal, such as oats and bran and pellets. They like whole grain bread too.
- Their favourite veggies are carrots, celery, spinach, cabbage and lettuce.
- They can have an apple or a pear once a week.
- And don't forget to fill the drip-feed water bottle every day.

When Tom had finished reading, his mum plucked the list from his hand, folded it and put it in her purse.

'You can come with me to the supermarket later,' she said. 'And then we'll go to the pet shop.'

Tom was silent as he watched his mother march towards the flowerbed in the back garden. With a bread knife in her hand she was poised ready to prune the roses.

'The people in my family are completely mad,' thought Tom as he made his way up the stairs and into the bathroom for a shower. As he left the kitchen, he noticed that his sister was still scribbling away.

Refreshed by the hot shower, Tom wrapped himself in a towel and walked to his bedroom. To his surprise, he found a note taped to the door, obviously penned by the girl his parents insist is his sister. Tom got dressed and sat down on the bed to read it.

Keeping A Rabbit Fit, Safe and Healthy

In order to save Muncher's life, I've decided to give you some more useful tips. But don't forget, onion breath, you owe me big time!

- Make sure there's lots of fresh hay in the sleeping area.
- Put cat litter or wood chips on the floor of the hutch.
- Place a bark-covered log in the hutch for the rabbit to chew.
- Rabbits should have their fur brushed every day.
- A rabbit hutch can be placed outside. But don't put the hutch flat on the ground. It could get damp.
- Don't put the hutch in the sun either. Rabbits don't like to be too hot. If it gets too cold, move the hutch indoors.

Tom placed the note on his bedside table and wondered how his sister knew so much about rabbits. After all, neither of them had ever had a pet before. Normally, Tom's first instinct was to ignore Anna's advice. Especially as she always had so much of it. But this time Tom was inclined to think that Anna actually knew what she was talking about.

'Okay, he thought. I'll spend today attending to Muncher's every need. But first I need some breakfast. I'm starving.'

Almost three hours later, and laden down with an array of packages, Tom staggered through the front door of the house and into the kitchen. Having just about survived an exhausting shopping expedition, and an insane, in fact, dangerous car ride with his mother, Tom felt relieved to be back home in one piece.

IT'S A FACT
Rabbits have strong, sharp teeth that grow all the time. They keep their teeth short by gnawing at plants and roots.

'Hugh, the car's out of petrol and there's a slight dent in the back fender,' mum called as she made her way into the kitchen. When no one answered she called again. 'Hugh, Anna, is anyone home?'

Tom ignored the silence that had just greeted them and began to unpack Muncher's food and bedding. Then he selected a variety of fresh veg for Muncher's lunch.

'Time to eat,' said Tom as he walked towards the hutch.

But there was no hutch. The hutch had gone. Tom glanced around anxiously.

'Mum, Muncher's ...' Tom began. But he paused mid sentence as through the kitchen window he caught sight of Anna and his dad perched on top of Mr Benson's fence. Not only that. Tom also spotted the rabbit hutch sitting in the centre of the lawn. The wire mesh door was open wide and Muncher was nowhere to be seen.

Tom raced out into the garden. 'What's going on?' he called to his dad and Anna who were by now rummaging around in Mr Benson's vegetable garden.

'We're looking for Muncher,' called back Tom's dad.

'Why? Where has he gone?' replied Tom.

'Well, Anna thinks he managed to get through the fence into Mr Benson's garden. And by the look of these lettuces I'd say she was right,' said Tom's dad from under a tomato plant.

'But how did Muncher manage to get out of the hutch?' Tom enquired. 'Well, Anna was letting Muncher have a run around. One minute he was happily hopping across the lawn, and the next he was gone,' came the reply.

Throughout all of this, Tom noticed that Anna was staying surprisingly silent.

It would appear, thought Tom, that his sister did not know everything about looking after a rabbit. Tom would have to think of an inventive way to point this out to her. But for now the

only thing that he could do was join in the search for Muncher.

Eventually it was Mr Benson who found Muncher hiding under a hawthorn hedge. Keen to remove his neighbours from his vegetable plot, he had joined in the search.

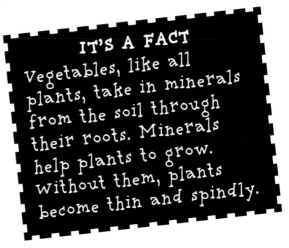

IT'S A FACT
Vegetables, like all plants, take in minerals from the soil through their roots. Minerals help plants to grow. Without them, plants become thin and spindly.

As Mr Benson handed Muncher over to Tom, his dad apologised for the damage – four lettuces and two cabbages. Mr Benson said that they shouldn't worry about it. Muncher had obviously been feeling a little peckish.

Back in their own garden Tom put the rescued rabbit in his hutch and fed him some fresh carrot. Then, after giving Muncher a stern talking to, he moved the hutch to a raised, shady place in the corner of the garden. Muncher responded with a number of nose twitches and settled down for a nap!

With the excitement over, Tom disappeared upstairs while Anna helped mum prepare the Mexican extravaganza she had planned for supper. Half an hour later, Tom reappeared. 'Who would have thought that taking care of a rabbit was such hard work,' said Tom, as he settled down to watch a video.

Moments later, Anna made her way to her bedroom to discover a note taped to the door. It read:

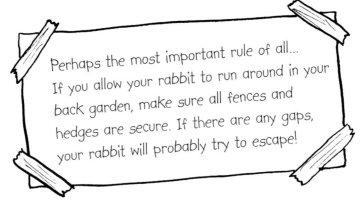

Perhaps the most important rule of all...
If you allow your rabbit to run around in your back garden, make sure all fences and hedges are secure. If there are any gaps, your rabbit will probably try to escape!

Three weeks had passed and Muncher had behaved like the perfect guest. Guest rabbit that is. And Tom, for his part, had fed, watered and exercised his little furry friend every day. In fact he had grown quite fond of the nose-twitching Muncher.

It was a sunny Saturday morning and Tom had just finished cleaning out Muncher's hutch when he heard a familiar voice.

'Hello Tom. Can I see de wabbit pease?'

It was Tom's three-year-old cousin Alex. Alex had arrived while Tom was busy attending to Muncher. He and his mum and dad were going to be staying for the weekend.

'Hello Alex. Muncher's in his hutch at the moment. You can have a peek at him if you like. I'll be letting him out for a run round the garden later. Then you'll really be able to see him. Okay?'

'Okay,' said Alex, who threw himself down on to the ground and pressed his nose against the hutch.

'Can he talk Tom? Can he say ...um, can he say ... chocolate buttons?'

'No, rabbits don't talk like people do Alex. But they do have their own ways of communicating. All animals do.'

'Oh! Well can he play football?' continued Alex determined to find out what rabbits do that he would find interesting.

IT'S A FACT
Rabbits sniff each other when they meet.

'No he can't,' said Tom trying to stifle a laugh. 'Rabbits like to play running and scampering games. Anyway, you'll find out all about rabbits this weekend because you're going to help me look after Muncher. Now let's go and find your mum and dad.'

Later that day, Alex helped Tom feed and exercise Muncher. He also cuddled him and when Tom wasn't looking he kissed Muncher on the nose – twice. Alex seemed pleased with his role as Tom's assistant rabbit keeper and that evening he chose *The Tale of Peter Rabbit and Benjamin Bunny* as his bedtime story.

'I like it when Peter Wabbit eats Mr McGregor's cawwots,' whispered Alex, as his eyes began to close. 'Muncher likes cawwots toooo!' And with that, Alex fell asleep.

As soon as Tom was sure that Alex was sleeping soundly in the spare bed next to his, Tom collapsed on to his own bed. He had come to the conclusion that looking after a rabbit and a small boy was very hard work!

Tom woke up to the sound of his mother and Auntie Jean, Alex's mum, laughing and joking in the kitchen. The smell of fresh coffee and toast made Tom feel hungry and with a great burst of energy he leapt out of bed. As Tom pulled on his shorts and a T-shirt, he glanced across at Alex's bed. But Alex wasn't there.

'He must have gone down stairs already,' thought Tom.

'Good morning,' said Tom as he strolled into the kitchen. Everyone was there, his mum, dad, sister, aunt and uncle. Everyone except Alex that was.

'Good morning Tom,' came the reply.

Tom sat down at the breakfast table and poured some cereal.

'Where's Alex?' Tom asked as he poured milk on his cereal.

'What do you mean, where's Alex?' Auntie Jean replied sounding more than a little anxious. 'I thought he was still upstairs asleep in your bedroom?'

Tom glanced at his aunt's worried face. 'Oh don't worry aunty. I bet he's outside in the garden with Muncher.'

IT S A FACT
A seed planted in a garden needs warmth from the sun, air and water to germinate.

Everyone went outside to have a look. But Alex wasn't there – and neither was Muncher!

'Oh my goodness, where are they?' exclaimed Alex's mum. 'Don't worry,' said Tom's mum, 'they can't have gone far.'

Earlier that morning, an excited Alex had woken up, his mind full of rabbit tales and adventures. And while everyone was asleep, he had decided to take Muncher to Tom's dad's allotment, which was just on the corner of Tom's road. There, Alex was sure they would find lots of nice things for Muncher to eat. And so, Alex, still dressed in his pyjamas, had attached Muncher to Tom's school tie and led the more than willing rabbit along the quiet, tree-lined street. Then, once inside the allotments he had allowed Muncher to roam free.

The allotments were well tended. Almost every vegetable grew there. There were potatoes, lettuce, tomatoes, beetroot, green beans and spring onions. Fresh herbs such as rosemary and mint, as well as an abundance of wild flowers adorned the edges of the vegetable plots. The allotments were also a haven to all kinds of wildlife. Thrushes, robins and blackbirds searched

IT'S A FACT
Allotments are a good example of a food chain. The vegetables are food for the slugs and snails, which in turn are food for the birds.

35

for tasty insects to eat. While the insects themselves dined on the vegetables.

Beneath one of the gardener's sheds, a fox had made herself a home. And underneath the hedgerow, a family of hedgehogs were sleeping off a busy night of searching for slugs and snails.

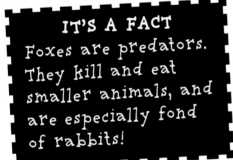

For a while Muncher had been content to hop about nibbling on the plants and vegetables, and Alex had been content to watch him. But then gradually both boy and rabbit had grown tired of these activities. And so, while Alex entertained himself digging up a small corner of the allotment, Muncher scampered off in search of new and uncharted terrain.

Almost an hour had passed but Alex hadn't noticed. (Not that he could tell the time anyway.) Suddenly he heard his mother calling.

'Alex, Alex, where are you?' As soon as he heard her voice, Alex ran to the allotment gate.

'I'm here mummy,' he called. Alex's mum ran and picked him up, hugging him tightly. Then, after a few moments of rather tearful silence, she said in a stern voice. 'Alex, you

36

must never do that again. You must never go off without mummy or daddy.'

'Muncher came too,' replied Alex.

'Muncher's only a rabbit darling. Now let's go back, everyone's worried about you.'

Tom eventually tracked down Muncher in the garden of a house near the allotment. Muncher had made his way there because he had sensed that there were other rabbits nearby. And he had not been mistaken. The children who lived in the house had two pet rabbits and Muncher had joined them for a scamper round their garden.

'You should be more careful,' the mother of the children told Tom. 'Rabbits shouldn't be allowed to roam around wherever they please. And don't blame me if your rabbit has babies either!'

IT'S A FACT
Rabbits give birth to live young. The mother feeds her babies on milk produced in her mammary glands.

'Babies,' Tom had said, quite startled. 'Muncher's a boy, he can't have babies.'

'Oh no he isn't and oh yes he can,' the lady replied.

Five minutes later, an anxious Tom placed Muncher inside his hutch. Then with the words 'don't blame me if your rabbit has babies' still ringing in his ears, he found a shady corner in the garden in which to contemplate the possibility that he might soon become an uncle.

'Oh boy, or should that be girl?' thought Tom. 'How am I going to explain this one?'

SCIENCE SUPERSTAR

Charles Darwin (1809–1882) was a very clever man. He discovered that although animals and plants appear to look the same from year to year, they are in fact changing all the time. And that includes us too! This is called evolution. Each generation of a living thing is slightly different from the generation before.

But how did Darwin discover this? Well, a lot of his ideas came to him as he sailed around the world on a ship called the *HMS Beagle*, visiting other countries to study their animals and plants.

Darwin observed that for many living things each day is a struggle for survival. They must find food and avoid being eaten. The more he watched the more he realized that those living things most suited to their environment had the best chance of survival. 'But what does this mean?' he thought to himself.

The conclusion Darwin came to was that plants and animals are able to change, or adapt, to suit their environment in order to survive. And that is why there is such an enormous variety of plants and animals in the world and why some can live in even the harshest conditions.

It also explains why some animals and plants have developed the most amazing ways of defending themselves, or hiding from possible predators.

Darwin published his theory in a book called *On the Origin of Species* in 1859. At the time lots of people disagreed with him and thought he was mad. But today Darwin's theory of evolution is widely accepted throughout the world as one of the greatest discoveries ever!

EXPERIMENTING WITH NATURE

Dear Reader

You are surrounded by living things and it's a lot of fun finding out about them. Plan your experiments in advance and think about what you need. Record the results in a notebook and don't be afraid to repeat an experiment if the results aren't quite what you expected. The following simple experiments are designed to get you out and about observing the world at large.

HOW OLD ARE YOU?

You can find out the age of a tree by measuring the circumference of its trunk. Most trees grow about 2.5 cm each year. If you divide the total circumference by this amount you will discover the age of the tree.

Measure the circumference of the tree at a point about 1.5 m above the ground. Then divide the circumference by 2.5 cm. Measure several trees and record your findings.

Who's been playing in my garden?

You might not realize it but all kinds of animals probably visit, or even live in, your garden or local park. Often they leave signs that they are around. Here are some to look out for.

1 Squirrels don't clean up after they have had a meal. Instead they leave chewed nuts and pine cones scattered about. They also eat tree bark.

2 Be on the look out for animal paw prints, pieces of fur, feathers and droppings. Use these clues to help you identify what kind of animal left them behind.

3 Listen carefully and you will hear birds trying to attract a mate, or telling other birds that your garden or park is their special territory! Try to spot their nesting sites but do not disturb them.

4 If your rubbish bin is disturbed, and rubbish is strewn around, you may have foxes visiting your garden at night.

Losing water

Plants take in water from the soil. Any water that they don't need evaporates through tiny holes in their leaves. Try this easy experiment to see for yourself.

Water a small pot plant. Put a clear plastic bag over the plant and tie around the stem. Leave the plant in a sunny place. After about two hours the inside of the bag will be covered with tiny drops of water.

★ LITTLE AND LARGE

Elephants are the biggest land mammals. They can weigh up to 6 tonnes and grow 3.5 metres high. But the largest animal of all is the blue whale. A blue whale can weigh as much as 80 tonnes and can grow to be 33 metres long.

The smallest land mammal is the tiny pygmy shrew. It's just 6 centimetres tall.

★ FAST AND SLOW

The slowest land animal is the sloth. If it moves at all it never goes faster than 1 kilometre per hour.

The fastest land animal is the cheetah. It can move at speeds of up to 110 kilometres per hour.

★ LONGEST JOURNEY

Arctic terns migrate from the Arctic to the Antarctic – and back again. In one year they fly more than 40 000 kilometres.

MIGHTY INSECT
Caterpillars have six times as many muscles as we have. They have more than 3000 muscles in their bodies.

HEAVYWEIGHT
The South American anaconda is the heaviest snake in the world. It weighs 200 kilograms.

MOST POISONOUS CREATURE
The arrow-poison frog from Costa Rica is the most poisonous animal in the world. The poison in its skin is so strong that one drop would kill a large mammal.

Don't Touch!

TINY FISH
The smallest fish in the world is the dwarf goby. It's just 15 millimetres long.

INSECTS GALORE
Did you know that there are more insects in the world than any other kind of animal?

★ MEAT—EATING PLANT

If an insect lands on a Venus flytrap, the leaves snap shut, trapping the insect inside. The plant takes two weeks to digest its insect meal.

★ BREAKFAST FRUIT

In Africa, there is a tree known as the sausage tree. It gets its name because the fruit of the tree looks just like sausages. The 'sausage' fruit grow up to 76 centimetres long.

★ PLANT SURPRISE

Do you know where rubber, chocolate, chewing gum, cotton, tea, cork, and perfume come from? Well, all of them come from plants that grow in different parts of the world.

★ COMING UP!

Bamboo grows faster than any other plant. It can grow up to one metre in a day.

MIND YOUR HEAD

The biggest seeds in the world come from the coco de mer palm tree, which grows in the Seychelles. Each seed weighs at least 24 kilograms.

WATCH OUT!

Guess what, there are about 500 different plants that eat animals!

WHAT A WHOPPER!

The largest living thing on Earth is a plant. It's a tree called a giant sequoia, or redwood. It grows in California, USA and has been given the name General Sherman. It's 84 metres tall and measures 31 metres round its trunk. It weighs as much as 700 fully grown elephants. It is more than 2000 years old!

PHEW, WHAT A PONG!

The rafflesia plant has the largest and smelliest flower in the world. It grows in the tropical forests of Asia. It measures 90 centimetres across, is covered in warts and smells like rotting meat.

GLOSSARY

CARBON DIOXIDE An invisible gas found in air.

CARNIVORE An animal that eats other animals.

CELLS The smallest units of living matter. Some living things have just one cell, but most plants and animals have huge numbers of cells.

CELLULOSE A substance produced by plants during photosynthesis. Plants need cellulose in order to grow.

CHLOROPHYLL The substance that makes plants green. It absorbs sunlight, which plants use to make food from carbon dioxide and water.

ENVIRONMENT The surroundings in which a plant or animal lives.

EVOLUTION The change in plants and animals over a long period of time so that they can survive in changing surroundings.

EXTINCT No longer existing or living.

GLUCOSE A type of sugar made by plants.

HERBIVORE An animal that eats only plants.

HIBERNATION The deep sleep in which many animals, such as bats and hedgehogs, pass the winter

INVERTEBRATE Animals that do not have a backbone.

LUNGS The parts of the body which an animal uses to breathe.

MARSUPIAL An animal that cares for its young in a pouch. Kangaroos are marsupials.

MATE When animals of the same species join together to breed and produce young.

MIGRATION The movement of animals from one area to another on a yearly basis.

NECTAR A sugary liquid produced by flowers.

NUTRIENTS Chemicals in the soil that are needed by plants to help them grow.

OMNIVORE An animal that eats plants and other animals.

OXYGEN A gas found in air. Plants and animals need to breathe oxygen to stay alive.

PHOTOSYNTHESIS The name given to the way plants make food from carbon dioxide and water plus sunlight.

POLLEN Tiny grains found in the male part of a flower. The grains must reach the female part of a flower in order to make a new seed.

POLLINATION When the pollen from the male part of the flower is carried to the female part of the flower.

REPRODUCTION The process by which plants and animals produce young just like themselves. A species that does not reproduce will die out.

SENSES The way that animals find out about their environment. The senses are sight, hearing, touch, smell and taste.

SPECIES One particular type of plant or animal.

SPORES Single cells that produce the female and male cells that are needed to make new plants.

STARCH A substance, like cellulose, that is made by plants during photosynthesis. Many foods, such as bread, pasta and potatoes, contain starch.

VERTEBRATE Animals that have a backbone.

INDEX

48